Love Reaches Out

In a world in which sex is so often exploited, the language of love has been blunted and coarsened.

Ulrich Schaffer puts thoughts into words that will help others understand and express their feelings. He explores with honesty and gentleness the delicate, developing relationship of those in love. His meditations reflect the singing joys, the sudden doubts of growing trust and love.

Ulrich Schaffer was born in Germany, and has lived in Canada since he was ten. He is now married, with two daughters, and teaches in British Columbia.

For Traudi

because most of these thoughts
began in the eleven years of ups
and downs we have so far shared.

We would like to pass on these
thoughts to others also engaged in
learning more about love.

Margie
Steve
Bill
Jeannie
Efis
Suzanne
Kirsten
Angela

An Aslan Book

Love Reaches Out

Meditations for people in love

by Ulrich Schaffer

Published by arrangement with Harper and Row Publishers Inc., New York
Part of this book was first published in Germany as *Ich will dich lieben*

LION PUBLISHING
121 High Street, Berkhamsted, Herts

First UK edition 1976

ISBN 0 85648 074 6

Cover photograph by courtesy of the English Tourist Board

Photographs by Tricia Porter (pages 8, 26, 82) and Sylvester Jacobs (38, 43, 58, 70, 93)

Text set in 12/13½ pt Photon Imprint printed by photolithography, and bound in Great Britain at The Pitman Press, Bath

Contents

Love is . . .

Foreword

In our noisy, shrill world our ears have been deafened and our hearts stunted. But hope remains; miraculously, we can still hear a soft voice when it speaks.

Speaking softly is one way of describing the poet's task. It is something Ulrich Schaffer tries to master. He writes with honesty and gentleness about love and sex in a world which has reduced them both to marketable products.

Today's generation is searching for reality and a sensitive way of expressing that quest. Ulrich Schaffer belongs to the new generation, and writes with openness and truth about the realities of living and loving.

Walter Trobisch

Love is:
daring to get to know

You liberate me

Never has anyone
given me the freedom
which you give me
—and therefore I love you.

Never was I allowed to be myself
among others
as much as with you
—and therefore I love you.

Never did I discover myself as much
as in the freedom
which you leave me
—and therefore I love you.

Fear of disappointment

I saw her again today.
We talked
and walked together for a while
and I am beginning to notice
the first signs of love in me
which send my head spinning.

I have to think of
the disappointment of my last friendship,
the uncertainty about my own feelings,
my immaturity which I always feel
  when I have to make decisions,
my insecurity
  which makes it hard for me to believe
  that anyone can really be interested in me.

And above all looms the fear
to be disappointed again
to be rejected
to be alone again
and to leave a part of my life
with another person again.

That's why I find it so hard
to really open up
to let others know who I am
and what I feel
—but I know so well
that no mature relationship can come about
unless I learn to share myself
and that is why I must make a real effort
right from the beginning.

I would like so much more
than a superficial relationship:
I would like to experience a love
that can change me and my world.

Jesus help me
to deal with my fears
to open up to her
trusting you and your guiding hand
in my lostness.

Love on the rebound?

You must help me come to terms
with my reason for loving you,
because I am afraid
that you are just a love on the rebound.

When he left me
just after I had centred my whole life
around him
it hurt terribly
and a void remained
—a feeling of being drained and ashamed.

Then I met you
and our love began
but now I am afraid that I am only loving you
to overcome the emptiness
in me.

And that would be so unfair to you
and disastrous for both of us.

Give me time and freedom
to search myself out
to look into myself
to find the motives of my actions.

Now

The beginning of a relationship
often determines
how it will continue
for the rest of its existence.

If we are willing to compromise ourselves
now
we will probably compromise ourselves later on.

If we don't talk about what's bothering us
now
we'll probably always try to avoid that subject.

If we accept a superficial love
now
we will probably have to accept it later on.

If we don't clarify our pasts
now
we will have to live with something separating us.

Let's begin right.
Let's give ourselves a chance
  even if it hurts now.
Let's not be afraid.
Let's be daring.
Let's be loving.

Unexpected fear

Suddenly I am struck by the fear
that I might lose you
and I quickly push away this thought
because I am afraid of the emptiness
you would leave behind.

But now I notice
how this fear makes me unable
to love you properly,
because inside me everything is cramped
and as I want to hold on to you
I rob you of all your freedom.

That is why I will fight this fear
and release you into a full freedom,
because I know that you can only come to me
if I let you go;
only then will you be free enough to be with me
without fear or a guilty conscience.

Then the miracle will happen
in us
and between us.

Difficult

How difficult it is
not to think about you
about us
and yet that is necessary
to do my work properly
to remain my own person
to love you.

I know there will always be times like that:
by not being with you
   I will be more with you,
by not talking
   I will be saying more,
by letting you be
   I will be loving you more.

Can you bear me?

Can you bear me
when I show you who I am;
when I tell you my worries
and the guilt that follows me?

Are you prepared to love me
even though you don't understand much about me?
Are you prepared to share my past with me
because it is also part of me?

Will you be able to endure
when you come to know that side of me
which is unknown to you,
which is hard to bear?

I cannot guarantee you happiness
but much pain
and much poverty
and much being-human
and much helplessness before God.
Therefore consider everything well
before entering into a deeper relationship with me.

Growing slowly

Please don't expect too much openness too quickly
because I can't give you that.
I would be skipping some important steps
and not heeding the law of slow growth:
everything that is to last
and to achieve a real depth
must grow organically and slowly.

I know of a man who planted a small tree
and because the tree didn't grow fast enough
he attached a pulley system to it
in the hope of pulling it up
and making it grow faster.

As he applied force
he tore loose the roots
which had just found their place in the soil
and were feeding the tree:
the tree withered and died.

We must be aware
that often we can't help love along
not even our own love
and that it must grow slowly like a tree
if it is to be healthy and strong.

My other side

I wrote to you yesterday
because I was frustrated
with what you had said the day before.

I did not want to mail the letter
until I had reread it today
because I wanted to see
whether I still agreed with what I had written.

Now I have reread the letter
and I realize that I reacted more strongly
than I would react now.

So I was ready to tear up the letter
but then I thought: why should you not see
what I felt yesterday?

I want to share as much as I can with you:
not just my happy friendly side
but all of me.

Realities

I am living in a fairyland.
My life is steeped in magic.
When I think of you
the world wears a glow
and you become my saint
complete with halo.

My friends laugh at me
and sometimes I stop to wonder
what is happening to me
—and then my wonderworld is pierced
and everything is shaken back into place:
into the world of realities
my friends tell me.

But again I have to wonder
whether the world of realities
is not the world of people
who have given up dreaming and hoping
for paradise,
who have lost the vision for the magic in life.

Perhaps those that talk of 'reality'
have lost the strength and desire
to sustain love, faith and hope.

Alone with you

Sometimes I am afraid
to be alone with you
because you might ask questions
and notice things
which I do not want to face
because I am afraid
that the beauty of our relationship
might dissolve.

Because when we are alone
I can not pretend any longer,
all distractions fall away
and I stand before you
and you stand before me
and I am afraid
that I will see something in you
that I will not like,
something which I do not want to see
because it might destroy the illusions
I have about you.

But just because of that fear
I want to be alone with you.
I will expose myself to my fear:
I want to see you as you are
and I want to show myself to you as I am.
I will subject our relationship to many questions
which might even separate us at first
but it is necessary
because fear will not let our love grow.

Come to me
as you are:
we want to learn about love,
love which knows fear
but is determined to overcome it daily.
Come to me.

In public

Even though we were alone yesterday
we are never quite alone
because others always share our friendship
and will share our marriage with us.

We belong to the people around us
and they belong to us.
We cannot shut ourselves off from them;
we cannot pretend that they don't exist.

In us all of humanity meets;
in us others can experience
  the miracle of becoming human;
in us others can practise their love;
in us God's love becomes visible.

Because of that
we want to let others enter our friendship;
we want to share our joy with them;
we want to make their suffering our suffering.

We must be honest before each other
and together we want to show others
how we live with each other
and spread hope that way:

the hope of love
and the hope of faith.

Pressure to marry

Please never think
that I am entering this relationship with you
because I don't want to be alone any longer.

I have seen too much loneliness in marriages
to believe that marriage solves that.

Neither does it bother me
that people are asking me when I will get married,
because most of their marriages
are not what I want.

I am also willing to bear the stigma
of being single
not even having a boyfriend
and I will not succumb to the pressure,
the sick pressure, of our society
that believes everyone should get married
or at least have a partner.

Let us throw all these reasons out
and find our own reasons to marry
or to stay single
—because we will have to live with our decisions.

In the beginning

Now that you have had to go away for a few days,
for the first time since I have known you
I can see you in my mind
—in your yellow summer dress
which you wore
when we met alone for the first time.

I was full of fear
and could not imagine
how we could talk for several hours
without running out of subjects.

And then everything was very different.
I talked about things
that I had never realized were in me
and I noticed your understanding.

I was glad to listen,
anticipating what you would say
and how you would react,
because that way I could see into you.

And already at our first meeting
I learned
that silence does not have to be embarrassing
but can be very beautiful
because you gave me the freedom to say nothing,
to simply share the silence with you.

All that is months ago now
and in the meantime our friendship has grown.
I feel so good being with you
and look forward to each meeting.

Jesus thank you
for the riches I have received in this exchange;
for the security I find in one person;
for the possibility to learn about love;
for my partner.

Your name

Hearing your name
frightens me sometimes
because I imagine
what I must mean to you.

Then I feel
that you mistake me
for the picture you have of me
to love me the way you do.

But then I realize
how much you mean to me
and I become very happy
and believe in our love.

Do I really love you?

I do not know if I love you
because I don't trust my feelings,
because I might imagine it all
and I don't know what your feelings are for me.
I do not know how to interpret your movements
but I wish that you would love me.

I am helpless
but I also know
that you cannot help me,
that I must decide alone
and then bear that decision.

That is why I am coming to you, Lord Jesus,
to ask for your help,
to ask you to sort out what is what,
what is happening in me;
to protect me from my fantasies
because I have never experienced
what I am experiencing now.
Never before have my thoughts been so much
with another person.
Never was I so confused.
Never so happy and so sad.

In danger

Do you know
that sometimes when I see you
I have to fight with pictures
that pass through my mind,
taken from magazines, films and books?

Then you become so cheap
and naked
and I have to fight
against the filth spreading out in me.

I notice the danger we are in,
how vulnerable we are,
and how much in need
of God holding us.

But in all this fighting
I love you more than ever
because I can sense a purity about you
that is a gift from God.

When I have to protect you
from my own imagination
you become so precious to me
and so pure.

Tell me

Consider yourself too valuable
to allow me to do
what you wouldn't want me to do:
tell me to stop
—because I must learn from you;
I must learn what your limits are;
I must know about your fears and hopes.

Perhaps you are more sensitive
and I can learn from you
but only if you guard your integrity
and teach me respect
along with love.

Tell me,
because I don't want to hurt you
by being ignorant
about your feelings and thoughts.

But you must tell me.

What really interests you?

It sometimes really bothers me
that you can switch topics so quickly
just when we are in the middle of something deep.

You just jump to unimportant things
as though our subject did not really touch you,
as though you were bored
with what I had to say.

Then I become frightened
because I notice that we don't meet,
that we just entertain each other
with thoughts and emotions
and I know that will not do for me
in the long run.

We will become shallow, uninteresting,
disinterested and boring
and we will drift apart
because we have not reached the depth
which could hold us together.

Shrinking heart

Sometimes I notice
that you become too important to me,
that you interfere with my being me
and with my relationship to God:

too important
because you have lost me
as a partner in dialogue
and you are left talking to yourself

—while I feel my heart getting smaller
instead of larger
as it always should
in love.

What went wrong with our love
if now it stifles us?

More than a good feeling

Soon we will reach the point
at which everything will become much harder
because floating in the clouds,
being blind
and pretending to be blind,
will have an end
which is especially painful
if we have not expected it
and we are caught unprepared.

Then we will know
what our love is made of
and whether behind our feelings for each other
there is the real will
to risk life together
and to endure.

Whether our caresses,
our words
actions and gestures,
were empty
and only a hidden self-love.

When we start to falter,
when we are torn apart by forces outside of us,
when we see the limitations
in the eyes of the other person,
when we know that we cannot jump
  over our own shadow,
then the test for our love has come
—love which is more than a good feeling.

We have to prepare ourselves for that.
We have to secure and anchor our love
now.
We have to train our willpower in forgiveness.
We have to see our own inadequacy before God
  and ask his help.
We must break through to a love
which comes from him
and which is so different
from our human capability to love.

Jesus
help us
again and again
to change our just being-in-love with love
to a mature and lasting love.

Love is:
changing and growing

Always changing

I know that I am saying the opposite
of what I said last week
but please don't hold me to last week
or last month
because I am always changing,
seeing things in a new light,
rethinking,
revising,
re-evaluating.

If I can't go on changing like that
I will die to our love.
If I have to adhere to what I no longer believe,
if I have to close my eyes
to new challenges and new obstacles,
I will be consistent but stagnant and dead.

I am unpredictable.
I cannot promise you anything.
I don't know what I will say next week
but
I have made the decision to love you,
to share my life with you
and to do that I need the freedom to change,
to remain alive in a creative love for you,
my love,
my friend.

Learning to see

I want to learn to see,
so that my blindness will become unbearable to me
and you will not have to go on being blind
to share my life with me.

It is in loving
that we learn to see
and in loving
that we become transparent.

Satisfied with too little

Let's not become like the couple we both know
who have nothing to say to each other,
who bore each other,
who are already dead without knowing it
and who have to hide their death
in being 'funny' and being 'pleasant'.

And yet twenty years ago
they thought they loved each other
and perhaps they did
—but didn't know that love must be nurtured
very carefully if it is to grow.
And perhaps they didn't know
that love can die
if not attended to;
that love does not perpetuate itself
like boredom does;
that love is fragile and vulnerable
and that only fragile love is strong.

Let's not allow our love to fizzle out
to be only companionship or sex,
or sharing a house, dishes and a car.

Let us work at our love
with the imagination that will sustain it.
Let's begin today
because tomorrow it will already be harder
if we have become accustomed
to not working at our love.

A different kind of love

I have known you for several months now
and the excitement of the first days is over
and sometimes I feel
that our love is dying.

But then I sense
a new love inside me,
a steady love,
a love not dependent on the ups and downs
of our fragile relationship,
and I become aware of a strong will
pulling me toward you,
a will to share my life with you
regardless of what might happen.

I am happy
that the excitement of love
is now giving way to working at love
and that a certain kind of being-in-love
must die
if love is to be born.

With every pain
my love for you grows
and the world changes around me;
the city opens up in a new way with you;
the books we discuss achieve a new meaning;
on our walks I learn to love
the things I neglected before.

My loneliness disappears
and is replaced by a new relationship
to the world around me,
because I have made contact with that world
by meeting you.

God's love for me
becomes visible in your hands
and I am changing
through you.

Standing before you, Jesus

Jesus we are before you:
when we are angry with each other;
when we kiss;
when we say what we expect of each other;
when we say that we don't want to meet any more;
when we discuss wedding preparations;
when we don't know answers to our questions any more;
when we talk about birth control;
when we look deeply into each other's eyes;
when we cry;
when we laugh;
we are always standing before you.

How good.
How frightening.
How encouraging.
How good.
How good.

Take our fragile relationship
into your strong hands
because we can destroy it so quickly
by carelessness,
by self-centredness,
by impatience.

Protect us from ourselves
and keep your love in us
when we want to live that love
as girlfriend and boyfriend,
as man and wife.

Others are watching us

I know that others are watching us
and thinking about our compatibility:
will she be good for him?
will he be good for her?

When I see them
I can imagine their thoughts
and I can sense
that their thoughts affect me.

We must watch and beware
not to live and do
what they expect of us:
we must decide in ourselves
what to do and what not to do.

It is difficult to be free
in an opinionated world
which attempts to make us all follow
the same patterns and conventions.

Daydreaming

I find myself writing your name
over and over again
and then cautiously
I write my new name under yours:

and I focus on our love
with every move of the pencil.

You are a secret to me

I know
that I don't know everything about you;
again and again you are different
from what I expected.

You are a secret
which enriches our friendship;
a mystery which cannot be solved
in a whole lifetime.

And because of that
I know that we will remain interesting
to each other
in the excitement of discovery.

Before I knew you

Before I knew you
I already had an image of what you should be.
I knew what your interests should be,
how you would move and talk,
and I saw myself at your side:
a cool couple
with style and taste.

Now I know you
and everything is so different
—but the image I had of you is still there
and I notice how difficult it is
to really meet you
as long as I hold on to that image.

When I notice
that you do not correspond to my image
I am sometimes surprised
that I still love you
because you seem like a letdown.

What a strange feeling that is:
I have to defend you against myself:
I list everything positive about you
as though I had to convince myself
that you are still worth loving.

But at the same time I know
that by changing you
you would not be you any more
but rather a dead picture
with which I would never be happy.

Then there are days
on which I am totally free of any image
and I can see you in a new way:
I can see how beautiful you are,
more beautiful than any image or picture,
because you are alive.

Stay with me
and do not turn into the picture-book girl
even if I seem to wish it sometimes.

Observations

1

How difficult it is
to know
what
I
am really thinking
when I think about you.

2

You are so different
from the person I knew
when I only knew you superficially
and yet
you have not changed much
you tell me.

Changing one's perspective
changes the world.

3

I wonder what I would sacrifice,
I wonder what I would do
for you,
if I were put on the spot

now.

4

Thank you
for taking the time
to get to know me

—I should do that.

5

If you see no faults in me any more
our relationship is in danger
because blindness has never aided love.

Sometimes I just play with you

I ask
without really caring to know the answer
because I am not interested
and I just do it
to give you a good feeling.

I say things
which I don't really mean
and about which I have not thought,
just to give you a good feeling.

I pretend to be with you
by slapping your shoulder
and smiling at you,
just to give you a good feeling.

Yet
really
I am playing with you
because I am not taking you seriously
and I am betraying you in a cruel way
and I am harming the relationship
which is just beginning between us.

I treat you like a thing,
not caring whether you cry or laugh,
whether you are lonely
or need to be alone.

When I play with you in this way
I destroy you more deeply
than if I tried to destroy you
because it is so difficult to react against
this subtle indifference
and even I hardly notice
that I am just playing with you.

I want to quit that:
want to stop my empty questions
and empty answers,
my meaningless sayings
and all the talk that avoids real issues.

I want to look into your eyes
and see beyond your eyes
where your riches open themselves for me,
where we are brought together by our seriousness
which liberates us
and lets us play in a way
that will allow us to see more deeply
into each other
than we ever could.

I will risk that love.

You are so colourful

The dream I have of you
and the person you are
are fighting in my mind
because I find it so hard to part with my dream.

I cannot see you as you are
because of the fear I have
of finding that you are different
from what I want you to be.

But when I awake
I realize
that you are so much more
than any dead dream
—more colourful than the black and white picture
I have always had of you
—more exciting than anything predictable
—in constant change and therefore ever new:
you are my love.

When I am with you

All that I can say
does not amount to very much.
All that I hear
is only a fraction of what is said.
And I see much more than my eyes see
when I am with you.

The river lays its meanderings
like giant ribbons at our feet.
The evening mountain
throws itself into a glowing for our retina.
Above the old afternoon
the rainbow blooms and renews my thoughts.

I can go for walks in your eyes.
I can bear buried secrets.
I can rest in your words
and become rich in the silence shared with you.
Even my hands and voice seem to change
when I am with you.

That which never existed
now becomes possible.

To own you is to lose you

When he comes,
the one you once liked,
then I ask myself
what position I occupy in your life.

Then I become unsure,
then I stumble over my words,
then you change and I change,
then I just want to be alone with you,
then I want to run away.

Then I would like to own you
so that I cannot lose you
and no one can take you away from me.

And yet I don't want that
because I know
that to own you is to lose you
and to give you up is to win you.

I won't say anything:
I will wait.
I can wait for you.
I can wait for your decision.

I will give you the freedom to decide,
because you,
and only you,
must decide,
you must find the way to me,
without my help,
without persuasive talk.

You must want to come to me,
and your will must be strong,
otherwise you will not find the way to me,
and you will become lost.

To become transparent

Have you noticed
that sometimes my face becomes dark
because I am hiding something,
because I am afraid to be exposed
and to stand open before you?

Sometimes I notice the same in you
because you also cannot confront the truth,
cannot bear to discover
how things are between us.

And therefore we lie to each other with silence,
we hide behind sayings with little meaning,
we flee into excuses,
we postpone our life into some future,
we stop decisive conversations,

we become strangers to each other
and do not share what moves us most deeply;
we become nontransparent,
we are fleeing from each other
and do not know how everything will end.

Let's stop doing that
and become transparent to each other.
Let us share our weaknesses and our strengths
to be free of each other and for each other
and so lift our relationship to another plane.

Forgiving

I know I should not have been so hard on you:
I should have overcome myself,
I should have forgiven you immediately.

But I couldn't.
Perhaps I did not want to
because I thought that some time had to pass
before we could be good to each other again.

How silly and shortsighted
because I know that time usually makes things worse:
dislike grows with time.
I always blame you and find reasons to justify it.
I know how to make myself look so innocent
and often time lets us forget
but it does not help
because nothing is forgotten that is not forgiven.
Time does not solve anything
because we need forgiveness and healing.

I want to forgive you
and ask your forgiveness
because I want everything to be clear between us
so that love can grow.

Believing in love

I love you unconditionally and more
deeply than anyone else in the world.
But I do not always believe in my love.
—M. Hausmann

I am becoming weak and sad in my love
because I am afraid
to become totally involved with you
—and yet
I cannot imagine a life without you.

I have taken you into my life
and I have moved into your life:
We have shared the ups and downs;
we have shared our innermost beings.

Any separation now
would be like a divorce,
even though we are not married yet,
because we have committed ourselves
to each other.

And yet there are two conflicting feelings in me:
my love for you on the one hand
and on the other my fear of this commitment
because sometimes I doubt our love
and our strength
to endure the hardships of a life together.

But I also know
that in every certainty
there will always be some uncertainty;
that moving close to another person
is taking a risk;
that opening up is a kind of dying
and that each marriage must be a trusting in God.

I want to take that risk:
help me to believe in our love
and help me to trust God
in all our failures
because in the end
only he
can sustain our love.

Alone

Without you I am so alone
but I know
that I must endure that
because I do not only want to come to you
to avoid my loneliness.

I know that is a bad reason
to meet and spend a life together.
I have seen so much loneliness for two.

Everywhere people live past one another
because they have not learned to share
and only want to exploit others
to escape from their loneliness.

I want to learn to be alone
in this time of separation,
to get a taste of being alone
and to learn from being alone
in order later to share with you
what I have learned.

I will use this time
to look into myself.

Waiting

I have told you so much about me
—you have seen me like no other person
—and yet sometimes I still hold back.

I know that you have noticed
how I occasionally weigh and ponder
whether I can say some things
and how sometimes
I decide against speaking
and I can see how that hurts you.

But there is no other way for me:
I must wait for the right moment
to say what I held back before.

Waiting is often the greatest part of love.

I don't want your sacrifice

I know that you were brought up
to think that you ought to sacrifice yourself
for the man in your life
but I do not want that:
I do not want your sacrifice
but your love.

If you must overcome yourself
to find your way to me
a dislike will slowly grow in you
and I will feel insufficient
and soon we will only be together
because we once began
and are now afraid to break off.

We cannot live that way
without becoming bitter.

Show me what you feel for me
and what you don't feel
and I will learn to respect this
and surround you with my love
in the hope
of turning your sacrifice into love,
in time.

Accepting you

Today I noticed
that I tried to talk you into betraying yourself,
into giving up your uniqueness,
God's gift to you,
because it does not agree with me
and is a problem to me.

Forgive me
because I want you,
I want to love you
without changing you first.

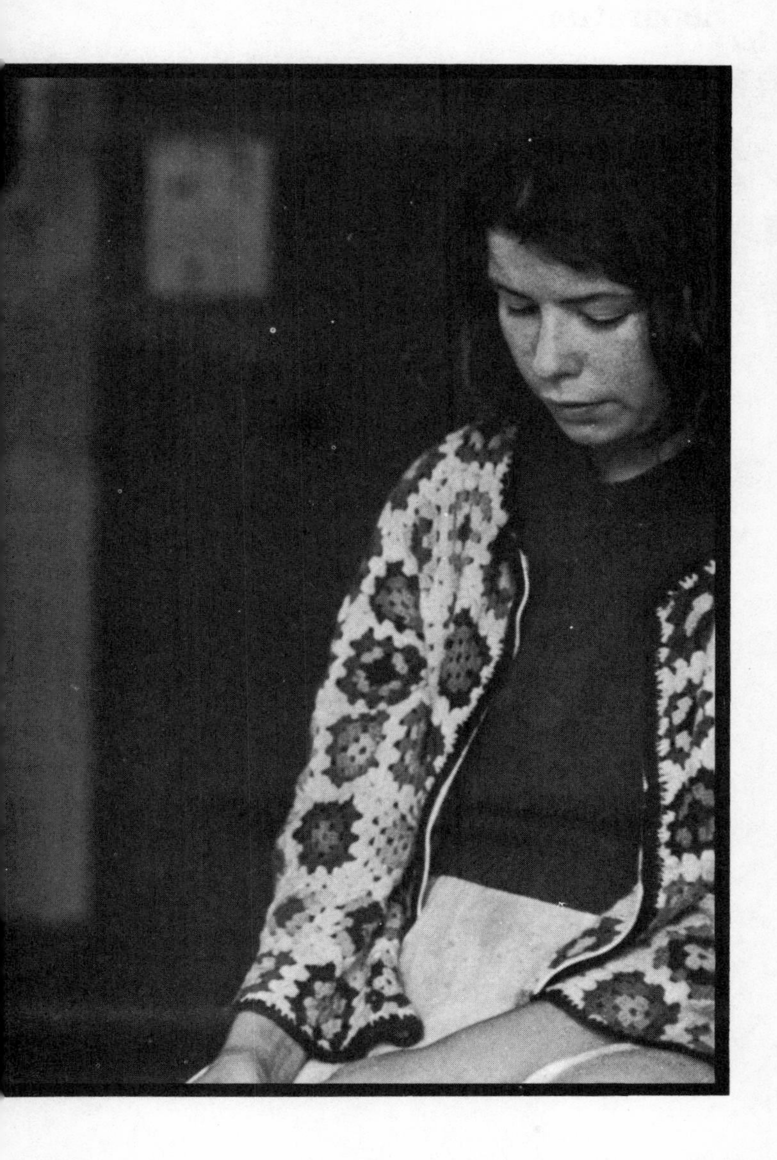

Separation

1

I know that you are very afraid
of the word *separation*
and yet we must talk about it
because I feel trapped
if I can't mention it.

Our relationship is so young and new,
so much at the beginning yet
that we must be free enough
to talk openly about our feelings,
to decide whether we shall go on
seeing each other
and to determine how we will meet.

If we take this freedom of decision
away from each other
we are fooling ourselves,
pretending to be closer than we really are
and building our relationship dishonestly.

2

I have watched so many people
begin relationships
and then continue them
simply because they were too afraid
even to consider splitting up;
too afraid of what people might think;
too afraid of the embarrassment;
too afraid of the anger of the partner;
too afraid to act clearly and honestly.

They did not even like the idea
of separating for a week or a month
just to have some time for themselves
to think everything over
and to reach a decision
one way or another
but without pressure.

And the reason
given for most of these actions was:
I don't really want to hurt anyone!
What would she think?
What would he say?

And they didn't realize
how they were already hurting each other
and how the pain was much bigger
when they finally did separate
or when they finally married
without really wanting to.

3

Please understand
that this does not mean
that my love for you has vanished:
it hasn't,
I still love you as much as before.

But I am sensing
that we are sliding into marriage
  rather than consciously deciding for it;
that we might get married
  because we haven't had the courage
  not to get married;
that we are beginning to take each other
  for granted
  without ever having reached the point
  of a definite and clear commitment
  to each other.

If this is so
we are heading for a dull life together,
a life without clarity and conviction,
without decisiveness and purpose.

4

If we believe in our love
we must not be afraid
to put the weight of separation on it,
to see whether it can take the strain.

I am not trying to break us up
but I need time to decide
and I need to be alone
in order to make up my mind
without the pressure of your presence.

Please try to understand
that I do not want to be a husband by default
and I don't want you to be my wife
because I'm OK,
not a bad guy,
or because you couldn't find anyone better.

I am disgusted by the average marriage
in which nothing happens
because it is no more
than two inert beings sharing the same space.

Never,
never,
do I want our relationship
to look or be remotely like that.

Repetition

Have you noticed
how we are repeating ourselves:

speaking in the same way,
doing the same things,
acting and reacting so predictably,
getting used to our love for each other,
getting into a rut
which is secure but uninteresting
and which will surely kill our relationship?

It seems as though we have known each other
for years already
when it's actually only months.

This must change
because without imagination,
without the drive to change and grow,
without the need to discover new aspects
in each other,
our relationship will die
and we will be like living dead.

We will be talking but not communicating,
sharing but not coming closer,
living but not growing.

Let me go

Sometimes I notice
how you get a hold of me
and I almost suffocate.

You approach me with expectations
which I cannot live up to
and in me remains the feeling of inadequacy.

You make demands
which I cannot fulfil
because it would destroy our tender relationship.

You believe you have rights in my life
but that way you take away my freedom
to give to you freely
because you demand
before I can decide to surprise you.

Let me go
so that I can come to you.

Love and sex

Jesus,
my friend and I live in a sex-oriented world;
we are exposed to sex everywhere;
everywhere your gift to us,
  the physical union as an act of love,
is made cheap: in films and novels
in advertising
and in the talking of people around us.

Everywhere sex seems to be more important than love
and for many love means just sex
divorced from responsibility
and from the decision to share life on a deep level.

All that is left is: make love!
and love is produced grotesquely
in one area of life and in one way
and few realize
that that can never be love.

We need you so desperately in this world
if we want to experience our relationship
as a gift from you
and if we are not to be washed away
by a wave of cheapness.

Help us
and teach us to wait for your time
before joining our bodies.

Parents

I am alone now
with what you have just told me
that your parents are rejecting me
and don't want you to see me any more.

They haven't even given me a chance.
They don't even know me
and I really don't know how to react
to their rejection.

I know that I love you
but I also know that I will be marrying
the family along with you
even if we live somewhere else.

And I must be certain that you will leave
your mother and father
to become my wife
and that you will not always run back to them
for advice concerning us.

From the day we decide to make our life together
our allegiances must first of all
be to each other:
only in that way
can we deal with the world around us
to which your parents and my parents belong.

Loving myself

When I love you more
than I love myself
I am really loving you less.

Loving myself less than you
I make it harder
for you to love me.

Your love for me
is so very dependent
on the love I have for myself.

And my love for you
will be stronger
if you love yourself the way you love me.

I cannot love

Jesus,
I come to you
because once again I am unable to love.

I have often produced love
within myself
but it never lasts.

I am coming to you
to be filled with your love
which reaches so much deeper than my love.

I am totally dependent
on the gift of your love,
the fruit of the holy spirit.

I can do so little,
only expose myself to your transforming love:
make me capable of loving.

Love is . . .

Love

1 Corinthians 13

Love is patient and kind:
  it still has patience
  after having said something a hundred times.
Love is kind,
envies no one
and is not jealous:
  it does not try to compete with another person
  it does not attempt to copy someone else.

Love is never boastful, conceited or proud:
  it does not show off;
  it does not say: look what I brought
    into our relationship!
  It does not emphasize its own achievements
  and it is not too proud to ask for forgiveness.
  It never says: without me you would be nothing!

Love is never rude or ill-mannered
  because the other person
  is always seen as a creation of God,
  as a thought of God.

Love is not selfish:
  you exist for him
  and he exists for you
  and you both exist for God
—only in that way will you find yourselves.

Love is not irritable or resentful.
Love is not quick to take offence:
It does not say: this is the last time . . .
if you do that again . . .
it forgives and persists.
It is not dependent on the love of the other.

Love does not keep a record of the wrong
of the other person.
Love can forget:
it gives the other person a new start;
it does not weigh down the other person
with prejudices and accusations.

It does not chalk up
words said in anger
and it does not use silence
to force the other to act.

It does not counter one wrong with another.

Love is not happy with evil
but is happy with the truth:
it does not cover up the wrong
but clarifies solves and forgives.
Love does not sell the truth
just to obtain peace.
It is never unjust
and for love there is no truth without love.

There is nothing love cannot face:
it can face the person it does not understand;
it can live in circumstances it cannot change;
it can face the inevitable.

Love believes everything:
it accepts the word of the other,
even if it is exploited at times.
Love is not ironic:
it means what it says.

Love has a limitless hope:
it does not give up hope for the other person
and when there is talk of a weak character
or of the power of heredity
love places God's powerful changing love
opposite to these.

Love endures everything:
it can bear the impossible;
it can bear the unjust;
and when everything in life seems to topple
—family, faith, profession and friends—
love blooms like a great hope
above the ruins.

Love will never come to an end.
Never will love come to an end.
To an end love will never come.
Love will never end.

Pain and love

1

Pain and love are twins
who often pretend
not to know each other.

2

The person who loves
will suffer
but not everyone that suffers
has loved.

3

My love for you
will cause you pain
just as there is pain for me
in my love.

4

If our love is to last
we must have a strong will
to endure pain.

5

To love someone
is to allow that person
to cause us pain.

6

All love is the yearning for perfection:
that is why love
causes our imperfection so much pain.

But love makes room for itself
through these pains
so that perfection can grow in us.

7

How painful
must our inadequate love be for God
who only meets us in perfect love.

8

When God's love meets imperfection
it causes pain
which is not the fault of love.

9

Unanswered love
is often not love
because love first changes
the person who loves
and is therefore its own answer.

10

All love for people
must at the same time
be directed at God

otherwise it does not reach anyone
and becomes unbearable
for the person loving
and the person loved.

11

The pain we feel
when we have more to give
than others can accept
is God's pain
with us.

12

To love someone
we must be willing to hurt that person
without making excuses
for our actions.

Often love can only be shown
by inflicting pain.

13

If you are disappointed in your partner
you have probably lived with an illusion
because it made life simpler.

It is never too late
to love the person you are with.

14

To fall out of love
into pain
is often the only way
to experience love.

15

Love and pain
both add immeasurably
to the completion of the world.

16

Even emotional and physical love
must have their core,
the spirit of God,
if they are not to become empty.

God either is
or is not
in every action.

17

Love is not the feeling
of a moment
but the conscious decision
for a way of life.

We want to love

Lord your love is death
because we have to sacrifice ourselves;
your love is punishment
which sets us right;
your love leaves us the freedom
to be evil.
Loneliness is your love and communication;
your love brings tears
at the moment of self-awareness,
before it is too late.

Your love is night and sun:
your love is the strangeness of the universe;
your love traps us
so that you can talk to us
finally
and only the cry to you is left,
the cry for your sustaining love.

Your love is the straight way;
your love is the detour of our life;
in every disguise your love is love,
always love.

We want to learn to understand you
so that we can see your love
and we want to love
so that we can see you.

We want to give ourselves away
  in order to grow
and we want to love
when we are not loved in return.

We want to love as a way of attack,
and a defence and sacrifice,
as gain and forgiveness.

We want to love
because God loves
and because he lives in us
when we love.

Other ASLAN Books include

Beyond Science
Denis Alexander

Doubt
Faith in two minds
Os Guinness

The Immigrant
Stories of an exile
Lawrence Dorr

Lord of the Air
Leary, Maharishi, Sai Baba, Jesus . . .
The personal account of a spiritual search
Tal Brooke

Mahalia
The authorized biography
of Gospel singer Mahalia Jackson
Laurraine Goreau

Tomorrow's Television
An examination of British broadcasting past,
present and future
Andrew Quicke